Wreaths for All Seasons

Wreaths for All Seasons

JAMES T. FARMER III

GIBBS SMITH

TO ENRICH AND INSPIRE HUMANKIND

For Mama—your love ever-winds and ever-circles all of us.
This is dedicated to you with all my love.

—James

First Edition
16 15 14 13 12   5 4 3 2 1

Text © 2012 James T. Farmer III
Photographs © 2012 by James T. Farmer III and Maggie Yelton, except
   Jacket front and back and pages 2 (lower right), 9, 12–14, 15 (upper and center),
      78–81, 96, and 118–127 © 2012 by Laurey W. Glenn, used with permission of
      the Time Inc. Lifestyle Group
   Pages 18–19 © 2012 by Torrence Photography

Published by
Gibbs Smith
P.O. Box 667
Layton, Utah 84041

1.800.835.4993 orders
www.gibbs-smith.com

Designed by Sheryl Dickert
Printed and bound in Hong Kong
Gibbs Smith books are printed on either recycled, 100% post-consumer waste,
FSC-certified papers or on paper produced from sustainable PEFC-certified
forest/controlled wood source. Learn more at www.pefc.org.

Library of Congress Cataloging-in-Publication Data

Farmer, James T.
   Wreaths for all seasons / James T. Farmer III. — 1st ed.
      p. cm.
   ISBN 978-1-4236-2487-5
1. Wreaths. 2. Floral decorations. I. Title.
   SB449.5.W74F34 2012
   745.92'6—dc23
                    2012012464

Contents

Introduction

When Granddaddy performs marriage ceremonies, he always gives the couple these words of advice: "The ring is an outward and visible sign . . ." An outward, visible sign—what lovely connotation for the description of a wedding ring. A ring—whether made from metal, fibers, flowers or foliage—has forever been a symbol of eternal devotion, a circle neither beginning nor ending. Rings may be seen as a mark and token of victory, the crowing glory of a championship match, race or athletic feat—looping souvenirs of accomplishment and note.

The vows continue, for the ring—the circle—is a sign, "of an inward and spiritual bond which unites two loyal hearts in endless love." The rings "represent something continuous, like the unbroken circle that they are, something beautiful and lasting."

I have always been fascinated by these words, by the imagery and symbolism rings represent. Hearing Granddaddy as celebrant, commissioning new couples with such thought-provoking words, leads my imagination towards other rings of symbolism and meaning—wreaths.

A wreath holds the same testament of never-ending devotion, while historically representing seasonal joys as well. Since the dawn of antiquity, wreaths have been used as adornment on doors, heads, tables, and homes. They are full of history, lore and representation. Take the name itself—"wreath"; it is reminiscent of our wrist's nomenclature, for our wrists, too, are circularly adorned with wreath-like hoops, twists, bangles, bracelets and jeweled entwinements.

So, from our wrists to our head, we wreath our anatomy; yet our homes become the true outward and visible sign of the fêtes of life, the joys of the seasons—the marks and representations of whom we are thrilled to greet and usher into our homes. Wreaths for all seasons herald the holidays, show signs of cordiality and hospitality, denote the glories of the present time and simply bring festive grace to each and every day.

We have seen them and used them in every season of life: to trumpet a wedding day, to hope all will be merry and bright, to wake up a winter day, to honor the harvest, to center a table, to announce the coming of spring. Whatever the season, celebration, holiday or event, there is a representational wreath. Our ancestors believed so too, for nearly every creed and culture has version of a wreath for some sort of notable day. Mt. Olympia's residents crowned their têtes for fêtes; ancient Europeans adorned their doors with grain-based wreaths to secure good luck for the harvest; Pacific islanders wove and still weave necklaces or leis of flowers to welcome guests; you may find them on doors and tables too. Wreaths and their various forms are timeless and culturally expansive.

Evergreen wreaths and those associated with the festive holiday times of Thanksgiving and Christmas make up a major portion of our wreath constitution. Lovely in symbolism themselves, their name and color suggest "ever living." From cypress to cedars, hollies to hemlocks, and to pines to podocarpus, evergreens abound across the land, readily yielding their foliage in the barren wintertime for the greenery we so long for during the brown and infertile months. It is as if there is a formula: evergreen wreath + swag or garland + tree + baked delights + twinkling lights = Christmastime. And if all that decking of the halls is too much to conquer, at least a simple wreath can don your door, giving your entry a cheery appeal for the holidays. The wreath finds its way not only onto doors during yuletide splendor, but mounted on walls, wired to gates, fashioned on windows, festooned onto mirrors, centering tableaux after tableaux, dangling from chairs and even spearheading grills on trucks (the latter I personally relish.)

Christmas and other High Holiday seasons do certainly retain a lion's share of wreath displays, but they don't have to be the only seasons for a wellspring of wreaths. Winter proper and its delicate serenity may be noted with a wreath of simple greens and barren branches. The verging vernal equinox may be harbingered with a wreath of eggs, flowers, fresh foliage or even nests. Summertime's heat yields a plethora of produce and plants for wreath making, and as the year winds down again, autumn brings us a true cornucopia of bounty to swathe the season with wreaths aplenty.

Join me as I journey throughout the year's distinct seasons on what I feel is always a concentric pilgrimage—a circular passage of constant searching for seasonal titivations. Trimmings for adorning my home,

bringing the garden inside, giving a nod to the season and celebrating each time of year with a wreath. All the while, my foraging and creating is in an attempt to make my friends, family and even myself feel the warmth that each holiday, season, and even day may bring.

As I started these words with recollections of Granddaddy and his homilies, I go forward now with my interpretation of the ring form, delighted to share wreaths from my garden, land, friends, family, and finds along the way. Be they traditional or twists on tradition, each wreath herein is a classic emblem of the circle of life. May you be inspired to grace your home with eternal, interlacing, ever-twining, never-ending signs of welcome to all those who enter—a wreath for each and every season.

Let's Start from the Very Beginning

Chicken wire, foam, straw, metal hoops and various and sundry other materials become bases of my wreaths. Each wreath has its own personality, and like personalities, each must be supported foundationally to fully form and spring forth.

Craft stores, floral shops, nurseries and garden shed finds all are my go-to sources for starting wreaths. I feel as if I'm always on the hunt for the right wreath form, the perfect base for my twining, crafting and concocting. Here are a few tips on wreath making that I have found helpful.

FOAM FORMS: If it is a fresh wreath of the garden's trappings, a foam wreath that can hold water will be best. The foam will be the font from which the freshly cut stems draw their water. Yet, if your garden gatherings are dried flowers, cones, sticks or even feathers, the foam form you use may be simply dry foam, into which your elements may be tucked and poked and wired. Foam is best for wreaths made of things that can be staked or are stemmed. The nature of this base works so well with cut flowers or accoutrements that a stake may be adhered to it. A stake and a hot glue gun are miracle workers!

LIVING WREATHS: Often, I find myself planting pansies, violas and even succulents into rings stuffed with planting medium, lined with moss, and secured with chicken wire. Planting the tiny plugs into these "living wreaths" makes a statement and is a fun way to garden—it is neither a plot nor a pot but a garden wreath! Sometimes I come across wreath bases actually made for this type of wreath. The soil is secured with a plastic covering and you poke the plugs through the cover and into the soil. If these are not readily available, then I craft my own.

Using a straw or foam wreath form, I cover the form with a piece of chicken wire, cutting the wire at the edge of the wreath as to halve the wire—imagine cutting a bagel or doughnut in half from the edge. These two pieces will then house the growing medium and moss. Line one half with moss and then fill the moss-lined form with potting soil. Secure the other half back onto the base half and plant your plugs or tiny plants through the holes of the chicken wire. Use moss to cover any gaps and to fill in holes—this helps to line or secure the soil. You may initially grow your wreath on a tabletop or flat surface and later hang it on the garden gate for a festive occasion or yard party.

STRAW AND GRAPEVINE WREATH FORMS:

Readily available at craft stores and floral suppliers, these forms are wonderful bases for adding greenery, dried materials and faux selections as well. By tucking the stems of the greenery into the straw wreath form (which is packed tightly and makes a great foundation) or the intertwined grapevines, the stems are secured. Of course, you may always tack, wire, glue, or fasten your wreath elements into these forms. These types of wreath bases are lightweight and can even be reused once the live material has faded.

STURDY METAL FORMS: These are the workhorses of the wreath form genre. It takes some serious elbow grease and even a hammer to flatten the metal prongs onto the stems and greens used to make this type of wreath. I recommend using these forms for heavy wreaths and large wreaths as well. If you are creating a wreath for a good-sized entry, this is the form to use. The clamping of the wire prongs onto the greenery gives it a grasp that's not going to let go! If you are handy with a hammer and have some patience, this form is for you. If not, many nurseries, florists and floral designers are available for hire to create this type of wreath.

Farmer's Favorites for Wreath Background Elements

Once you have decided what type of wreath you are making and the form you are using, consider these traditional and twists-on-traditional materials for your greenery.

Cedar

Cypress

Pine

Magnolia

Boxwood

Eucalyptus

Podocarpus

Pittosporum

Fraser Fir

Acuba

Spring Fever

As if a trumpet has sounded out of the austerity of winter, spring bursts forth from its predecessor in an amazing range of sounds, colors, and textures. Birds and bees long silent are now cacophonous and buzzing. Grays and browns have yielded to green—vibrant spring green—and a myriad of tones, hues, and shades now dot the landscape. Frilly fern fronds, leafy shoots, budding branches, soft and downy grasses all emerge, giving the garden texture. Let us now celebrate, herald, and truly delight in spring. Wind and twine a wreath for this season with the festive elements now at hand.

WEDDING DAY BLISS
A grapevine base is
completely covered with
magnolia, hydrangea and
"bridal wreath" spirea
tucked into the form. This
type of spirea has long
been used in the South
for spring weddings and
makes a gorgeous wreath
in and of itself. With its
arching growth pattern,
the blooming branches
are nimble enough to
wind together to form
a wreath or to accent
one, as I did for my dear
cousin Sally Kathryn on
her special day.

SPIN A YARN FOR SPRING This wreath nods to springtime with cute craftiness and also alludes to nature with flora and fauna touches. Spring-green yarn is wrapped around a small foam wreath form. Creativity can abound here with the style and fashion of the wrapping. A nosegay of spring blossoms and garden greens—camellia, viburnum, pittosporum and fern frond—is affixed to the wreath as a brooch might be attached to a hat. A faux bird's nest casts our gaze towards spring and picks up on the colors beginning to blossom in our yards.

SEEDPODS AND CONES—I love to use pine-cones as accents and entire wreaths too. Lotus pods are a favorite as well.

FUNGI—Preserved shelf mushrooms, lichens, and sponge mushrooms are available at most craft and floral suppliers. These make a fantastic addition to any wreath or as a wreath themselves!

BERRIES—Holly, eucalyptus, privet, ligustrum, beautyberry, rose hips, nandina, "popcorn" tree and more are marvelous choices for a wreath.

SEASHELLS—Whether a wreath is made totally of shells or accented with a few, I love this nautical nod, especially during the summer months.

FOUND OBJECTS—A bird's nest, a wasp nest, twigs with moss, old pulleys, bits of driftwood, or a feather or two make your wreath personal and personable.

Be creative with your wreath greenery and pops too! Let the seasons speak to you and inspire your creations.

Color and Pizzazz Elements

Any of the aforementioned wreath bases themselves are lovely signs of the season, but try another step to add a bit of pizzazz. Adding the "pop" elements will make these wreaths come to life and deliver some personality too.

FRUIT—sugared, sliced or dried. I love using fruit on wreaths. Often, the inside of the fruit is just luscious in flavor and color appeal; so slice open that pomegranate or grapefruit and show it off!

FLOWERS—All one type of flower—such as roses, carnations, hydrangeas or lilies—or used as an accent. Dried flowers are great too, giving us mementos of the previous growing season.

HERBS—rosemary, lavender and sages look great fresh and dried for wreaths. Try a wreath of all dried lavender—it will be divine! Cinnamon sticks are aromatic add-ons too.

Palmetto

Bay Leaf

Laurel

Oak Leaves

Ivy

Folded Aspidistra Leaves

Anise

Camellia

Wheat

Moss—mood, green, Spanish—all work as a wreath
on their own or as accent.

GREEN DELIGHT A myriad of mosses constitutes this wreath. Clusters of mood, sheet, and Spanish are hot-glued onto a foam wreath form. "Chrysanthemum lichens," as I call them, are also tucked into this arrangement of multilayered and multicolored green mosses. Sometimes a wreath of all one color or varying forms of a single variety of plant material is just what is needed.

BURLAP AND MOSS In the floral design industry, we have a saying, "Burlap and moss can cover a multitude of sins!" They can also create beauty when combined. A wreath of all sorts of different mosses with burlap woven throughout makes a statement in any season. The winding burlap weaves movement and rustic texture throughout the wreath, while the various mosses add the natural earthen element. Whether as a chic combo on its own or as the base on which to build a highly seasonal wreath, one can never go wrong with this pairing.

LIVING WREATH OF JOHNNY JUMP-UPS

Whether you are just craving a new niche for gardening or are limited on garden space, a living wreath just might be the wreath for you. Planting pint-size pansies, violas, or even "panolas" (a pansy/viola cross) in a snuggly bed of moss and rich potting soil will give your garden gate a peppy swing each time you and your guests enter the garden.

Violas, in particular, fare well in this sort of wreath form, for they bloom profusely and even trail, spill and fall from the form, giving movement and rhythm to the wreath. Of course, like most wreaths, this one makes a terrific centerpiece and tabletop arrangement. Pick out your favorite color combos, plant a mixed batch and be amazed at the sheer joy a living wreath can bring.

Farmer's Faves for Living Wreaths

Pansies, violas, succulents, begonias, huechera, portulaca, sedums, creeping thyme, Ajuga and dwarf mondo too!

ARTICHOKES APLENTY Constructed on a foam form, this wreath of preserved artichokes and hydrangeas makes a wonderful statement. A great gift for any gardener or chef, this wreath's plays on chartreuse, jade, and lime green meld together, for a visually delightful wreath. Sometimes unexpected combos are just the ticket to a fabulous wreath. Remember, moss covers a multitude of sins, so tuck moss into gaps and use as filler for added texture and pizzazz.

HERE COMES THE BRIDE Green and white is the classic combo to pair for a wedding—a crisp palette for any season but delicious as a spring duo. Here a foam wreath is covered in dried hydrangeas and accentuated with white roses. A winding ribbon of netting coated in moss finds its way to the top of the wreath, where it is fashioned into a bow. Hanging a wreath such as this is completely traditional for any wedding, and the moss netting gives a garden twist.

Since roses and hydrangeas can be dried, this wreath may be preserved and theme an entire season, donning the doors of not only the church or ceremony site, but also beautifying a home or other venues for engagement and anniversary parties to come.

EGG AND VINE I truly adore Easter and the décor that is synonymous with this most wonderful holiday. Earthy taupe, lavender blue, duck-egg green, speckles, spots and creams and whites—eggs come in a myriad of colors and sizes. Using eggs for an Easter wreath is highly symbolic: eggs represent new life, expressing so elegantly the Easter season and spring. I love using wreaths on the doors of armoires and my buffet deux corps for an unexpected pop of seasonal fun. The faded French blue patina of this piece and the adorable pastels of the eggs are truly heartwarming.

Wiring, gluing or staking real eggs to a wreath form is akin to nailing Jell-O to a wall! I love to use faux eggs in various shapes, sizes and finishes for this wreath and spring décor. Rarely do I use artificial materials for my décor, but this wreath is an exception. These eggs are so lightweight and easy to adhere to the rustic grapevine base—and since it's artificial, I can reuse this wreath every year.

Some plugs of faux sedum tucked in with the eggs gives the pale pastel complement and added texture to the eggs' color scheme. For further drama and movement, I like to twist additional pieces of the grapevine—an outward indication of the wreath's base.

Summer Everlasting

Spring's delicacies fade and harden into strong stems. Plots of seedlings become rows of constant produce as the heat waxes. Green is abundant and the gardens are full of flowers, fruit and foliage. Wreaths for this season may boast the best of this garden's fullness. Slip a wreath over a garden gate or hang it on a tree trunk where everyone will see it as they stroll by. Or set tableaux of summer posies and such en plain air to decorate your porch or patio table with the emblems of this season. May your summertime wreaths be reflections of warmth, visible signs of the outward grandeur this season bestows.

PALMETTO PRIDE With a backdrop such as the May River in Bluffton, South Carolina, a wreath made entirely of palmetto fronds on a wired wreath base welcoming boaters to this dock is completely apropos! South Carolina's state tree is the palmetto, and with good reason: forests of them grow all over the Lowcountry and even into the midlands of South Carolina, Georgia and Alabama. The shorter, more shrub-like palmetto grows wild along the banks, swamps and sloughs of my home's native river, the Ocmulgee. I relish any opportunity to decorate with these gorgeous flora specimens and a wreath made from them is a true treasure.

LAVENDER AND ROSES Set on a bed of dried hydrangeas, this wreath is accented with fuchsia roses and dried lavender stalks. The aroma from this wreath permeates the air and is a welcoming enticement to anyone fortunate enough to pass by. Traditional ingredients in potpourri, these elements are instant classics for a spring or summertime wreath. Hanging on an old stained glass window at my aunt and uncle's home, the colors all meld together for a charming display of floral art and lovely architecture.

LAVENDER LUXE

Wreaths constructed of all one material, or *en masse en Française,* are so simple and *trés chic*! With lavender reminding me of my journey to Provence, this wreath is just a mere sniff and smell away from that trip. Nostalgic for such a lovely place, I clamped together small bunches of lavender on a wire form in a clockwise manner to create this wreath. Lasting well throughout the season, this wreath may grace your home for months. As the stalks dehisce—dry out and shed their flowers—you may save the lavender granules for potpourri.

FUNGI FUN This wreath is made entirely of preserved sponge mushrooms. I adhered a stake to the back of each mushroom with hot glue and literally stuck the preserved fungi into a foam form, arranging them in a concentric pattern, then dotted the holes with mood moss.

LES JARDIN DES FLEURS
Dried flowers meld together to form a wreath with rhythm and cadence. The pops of color from dried gomphrena, clover, yarrow, larkspur and hydrangea gather in a cheery mix on this wreath. Since the flowers are all dried, gluing them to a foam form was easy and created a cropped, elegant feel for this wreath. Here it sits in a field of rye grass and awaiting a jaunty ribbon to be tied and bowed. Moved closer to home, a wreath such as this will warmly welcome your guests.

Raw silk ribbon lined with a bit of wire is a marvelous accoutrement for any wreath. The texture of the raw silk is reminiscent of the dried flowers, and the bit of wiring gives the ribbon strength and body. Colors such as these—corals, salmons, yellows and creams—are highly amusing on a wreath with similar colors but amazingly beautiful on a simple wreath of one element too.

PRESERVED PROMISES

When my cousin Gray wed his sweetheart, Jamie, the day couldn't have been any hotter! A family wedding at our country church was just the spot for the nuptials, and wreaths to handle the heat were in order. Preserved boxwood forms are elegant year-round, and the dried hydrangeas were a memento from the passing blossoms the shrubs gave us much earlier in the summer. Silk ribbon of bridal white elegantly ties the hydrangea bundles and gently adds another texture to the wreaths. The happy couple may enjoy these wreaths as preserved tokens of the special day they made their promise vows.

Autumn Delights

The swan song of the seasons—the last hoorah for the

garden and nature—autumn is upon us and glorious

delights thrive and flourish in this time of contrasts. Trees

lose their fullness but yield crops of cones and nuts in

their dehiscing. Flowers blossom and dry. Greens turn

to gold and orange and scarlet and rust and aubergine.

Materials must be used, for winter will remove them. The

time is nigh to gather all these glories and make each day

a festive reminder of this enchanting season. Now we may

fashion wreaths with gourds, cotton, leaves, nuts, dried

flowers, seedpods and vines. Harvest time is upon us, and

this is the time for a wealth of wreaths.

BOXWOOD AND BURLAP Greens and browns abound during the fall and winter in various shades. Boxwood, the American box in particular, has a lush, deep green cast that pairs well with so many things. A formal greenery, in my opinion, the contrast of boxwood with the rustic burlap ribbon meandering through the wreath makes for a charming combination. Punctuated with pinecones and some preserved lemon leaf, this wreath is totally apropos from late autumn through the holidays and well into winter. With what better kind of wreath than this can you welcome your friends?

Probably one of my favorite attributes about wreaths is that they are not limited to doors. I especially love the opportunity to use them as centerpieces—even more so on a round table. The concentric circles of the table and wreath are quite fitting, and the center is perfect for a hurricane and pillar candle.

PULLEY PLEASE Who says a wreath must be constructed of garden material? A friend gave me this wreath for Christmas (as is the nature of wreaths, they make lovely gifts). She had some rusty old pulleys in her barn and wired them together, adding the frill of a burlap bow and *voila!* Now my imagination began to reel: what else could I make into wreaths? Twine, rope and yarn came to mind but also driftwood, shells, old spools, and a myriad other parts and pieces.

Let your creativity be inspired by piles, buckets chock-full of things, and rusty pulleys—you may have a fantastic wreath in the making!

GOURDS AND POPCORN The wreath form itself is charming: a wiry, twisting array of willow sticks and small branches seem to mimic a sunburst mirror. Adding any items to this wreath is simply gilding the lily. The popcorn tree (*Sapium sebiferum*, or Chinese tallow tree) is widespread across the Deep South. Many folks think of it as a "trash tree," but I think the nearly heart-shaped leaf and fall color are nice and the fruit is marvelous for decorating.

Take this wreath, for example: mixed with some small gourds and seedpods, it can spice up a chilly winter's day and usher in any crowd from the cold. One man's trash is another's treasure, and the popcorn berries are a treasure to me!

FALL INTO WINTER I love this wreath. My great-grandmother had a pinecone wreath on her door during the wintertime that was slightly shellacked. In fact, Mema shellacked and gold-painted most anything of decorative value! The slight varnish on some of these cones and the mix of their shapes and sizes is simply splendid for this wreath. The cones are staked and stuck onto a foam form, which moss helps to hide. Lotus pods, too, add texture and tonal interest. This wreath can ring in Thanksgiving, Christmas *and* New Year's Eve. A quick switch of the ribbon dresses it for the particular holiday soiree. The dried orange slices give a touch of lusciousness to the wreath as well. Orange and brown are sharp colors for the late autumn time and through winter.

THE PLEASANT PHEASANT Basking in the delightful mix of a mélange of greens, this wreath consists of artichokes, Cryptomeria and ivy—all wired to a Fraser fir wreath base. The tiny ivy leaves wind their way around the pinecones and artichokes set in an organic approach. Pheasant feathers flit in a flurried fashion, giving this wreath a pop of character and personality.

If red is not your color but you need a festive note from Thanksgiving into Christmas, try this wreath. It looks great on the winter scene as well, and the artichokes may be eaten once they have served their aesthetic purpose. Texture and tone run hand in hand with this wreath; the feathers simply dress it up for sheer enchantment.

A FEATHER IN YOUR CAP A wreath form of clipped willow branches is expanded upon with preserved bay, yarrow, artichokes, lemon leaf and various seedpods. The pizzazz, fun and drama comes in with the radiating pheasant feathers branching forth from the wreath's outer circumference. The feathers spin from the wreath, creating a clockwise motion with terrific effect. Akin to a windmill, this wreath with its feisty feathers is perfect for an autumnal fest. Whether you are decorating your door, barn, potting shed or home interior, a wreath such as this provides whirling delight for the senses. How does a lady spice up a hat? Stick a feather in it! The same proves true for a wreath.

WELCOMING WHEAT

Tried and true, wreaths of a single element *en masse* prove to be dramatic, simple and elegant. A green field of wheat is one of the most beautiful sights to me, rivaled only by a golden field of the same grain. Whether green wheat or faded gold, in the field or as a wreath, I surely take solace from the sight of wheat. Adorning the tractor or your door, this style of wreath is classic for the fall months and makes a great base also for creating other wreaths. The clockwise motion of wheat sheaths bundled around a wire form will always rank high as a true favorite of mine.

AUTUMN GLAM What says "fall" better than glorious leaves in shades of autumn's best? Take those leaves and create a wreath for one truly glamorous element of décor. Massed and adhered to either a wire from or grapevine round, or even glued to a foam form, fiery colors of gold, orange, sienna and terra-cotta as well as flashes of burgundy all meld together for this wreath. For added movement or rhythm (I feel every wreath needs some sort of cadence), try weaving in strips of burlap. Preserved leaves, dried leaves from seasons past or freshly fallen foliage all stand as super choices for a wreath celebrating of the grandeur and glam of autumn.

CORNUCOPIA'S DELIGHT Spilling forth as from a cornucopia itself, this wreath bursts forth with the elements of fall. Gourds, lotus pods, leaves, dried loquats and pomegranates, and a cacophony of other pods and textures all combine for a festive and amusing way to herald, celebrate and welcome the season. By using varying textures, shapes and sizes of the materials, dimension and complements work hand in hand for delightful design. Adorning a favorite tree to welcome autumn—or a door or table's center—this wreath is sure to bring the season into your home and garden with flair. Warm, earthy tones of maize, rust, copper and sepia play off the textures and shapes to further enhance to feeling of fall.

NATURE'S NEUTRAL FOR FALL Green is nature's neutral color. The color is found is many different hues and tints, and paired with white this classic combo has its varying elements for each season. For fall, I like to take a boxwood wreath of fresh or preserved greenery and wind in dried lambs ear and dusty miller. Dried décor for fall is totally in sync for the season, but this take on autumnal style with these components gives us an opportunity to celebrate in a different fashion. Maybe it is a fall wedding, a shower perhaps or just a twist on traditional schemes, green and white combos are at home in any season.

COUNTER EFFECT FOR FALL

Nothing like taking elements of a season and twisting the design a bit, creating a spin of the season's décor—literally! By crafting this wreath in a counterclockwise fashion, a spinning effect gives personality and even a rhythmic note to this form. Dried okra pods, grasses, feathers and moss set on a clipped willow base are woven against the clock, and yet it is still quite visually appealing and seasonally grand. All the elements being linear further creates the cadence this wreath portrays—an ebb and flow of materials. The inner circle of green moss anchors the center, giving the wreath a pivot to spin in this reverse manner.

GOLD AND BROWN FOR COUNTRY OR TOWN Made entirely of elements in the vein of varying gold and brown hues, this wreath is at home on the farm or on a city door. Highly festive for the fall season, a collection of lotus pods, pheasant feathers, various seedpods, ochre-tinted artichokes, rust-colored leaves, deep auburn yarrow and willow form a wreath of amazing autumn enchantment. Complements abound with smooth pods and rough-textured ones, crispy leaves and silken feathers. Shapes, too, interplay to create depth and dramatic staging for the perfect wreath for fall. The absence of any green further denotes this wreath as a high autumn piece, thus reinforcing a design mantra of keeping tones together for elegance and form.

Winter Welcomes

The cymbals of nature's orchestral tempo crash upon Christmastime, ending the growing rhythm of nature's cadence. Our homes, filled with the fullness of seasons past, dissolve into the solace and serenity this season imparts. Such sentiment may be reflected in the wreaths we create. Evergreens lend their lusciousness, doubling their demeanor with scent and aromatic pleasure. Cones from evergreen conifers now, too, become our winter thrill and help ward off the winter chill. Moss-covered branches and naked vines remind us of foundation and simple shape. The elegance of winter's simplicity can be matched in its celebratory wreaths—gentle reminders of hope and longing for the seasonal cycle to begin anew.

FOUND FLORA AND FAUNA Since childhood, I have picked up and carried home trappings and trimming from my forages into the woods on our land. It may be an interesting feather, a rock with character, or a particular stick. My forays would always yield something of note, and I found that wreaths were a perfect form for displaying my finds. For this wreath, a wasp nest, some popcorn berries, fern fronds, my favorite magnolia and some *Agarista,* or Southern pipe plant, all perform in harmony as tokens from this particular walk in the woods. A willow branch form serves as base, and the finds are literally tucked directly into the tightly woven sticks.

WINTER WONDERMENT Cones and seedpods of every shape and size make up this wreath. Built on a wire form for sturdiness, each and every cone, seedpod and fiber is wired to the base. A touch of red and gold paint delicately and sporadically applied here and there gives some contrast to the deep browns and sepias this wreath displays. A festive ribbon can take this wreath from season to season, holiday to holiday. Varying sizes, shapes and textures give movement and character to this wreath and a bit of personality too.

STICKS AND CONES

Winter's austerity can be shockingly beautiful. To my eye, this wreath exemplifies the serenity of a winter's day. A wreath form made of willow branches and interlaced with sticks, various-sized pinecones and dried oranges makes such a statement for this entryway. Though the season is chilly, warmth is exuded from this wreath, this entry, and in turn, this home. The earth-toned hues and tints of the materials, with just a glimmer of glittery gold, are enchanting. Since the materials are preserved or dried, plan on using this wreath for many seasons to come.

BOXWOOD BOUNTY As winter lulls onward, we become so appreciative of evergreens. A stalwart in this field is the boxwood. This wreath is made from preserved boxwood clippings and may be arranged in either a clockwise or counterclockwise pattern—giving a swirling motion to the wreath. Movement created by the positioning and placement of the materials on the round wreath forms is a key element to creating a memorable wreath, even if the wreath is only made of a simple evergreen.

GARDEN SUNBURST
A radiating rim of
pinecones makes this
wreath appear like a
sunburst. The glimmer
of the glittery gold lotus
pods helps it shine,
while the chartreuse
moss sets off the browns
and golds. Preserved
sponge mushrooms
give depth and add a
third dimension, too,
as they protrude from
the wreath's refined
dimension. Whispers
of dried 'Limelight'
hydrangea further add
to the ephemeral feel
this wreath conveys and
reminds us of summer's
great floral bounty from
seasons past. Shades of
brown, hues of greens,
and pops of gold are
sharp and handsome
combinations to ward off
the dreariness of winter.

WILLIAMSBURG EVERLASTING
The charm of historic Williamsburg has never left my mind since my first visit. It was wintertime and it was cold—much colder than this Southern boy had ever known; yet, I was warmed by the use of fruit and foliage for the wreaths—the bits of spice and special materials that gave their décor personality.

This is my take on Williamsburg style—recognizable items such as boxwood, pinecones, dried pomegranates and dried oranges but livened up a bit with sponge mushrooms, moss and cinnamon stick bundles. Using a mix of preserved and fresh materials makes a hearty and attractive combination. Since so much is preserved in this wreath and the boxwood dries well, I can have Williamsburg Everlasting for years to come.

POMEGRANATE PIZZAZZ The pomegranate dons the coat of arms of my mother's family, the Granades. My affinity for pomegranates is stronger, I feel, because of our crest. Yet, even if the pomegranate were not a symbol of my family, I would be enamored with the fruit for its sheer beauty—inside and out! Here I took varnished, dried pomegranates and affixed them to a foam form, working in a concentric circle for the outer edge and trying to follow suit moving toward the center. No two pomegranates are the same, so the circular pattern is not perfect; a little moss fills in where a pomegranate will not. A brown-and-cream-checked burlap ribbon and bow holds this wreath and welcomes not only the Granades to our home but all who enter.

ALL THAT GLITTERS IS GOLD

My great-grandmother, Mema, had an affinity for gold décor—spritzed, sprayed, painted, dusted, dipped or maybe even draped in gold lame. After a wreath, for example, had faded or browned, all it needed was a little bit of gold paint. "There was never an old barn a little paint couldn't hurt." This was Mema's mantra.

As an homage to her and, truly, a bit of relish for myself, a wreath of all gold elements came to be. Salal or lemon leaf, lotus pods, pinecones and birch twigs all melt together into a lovely pot of gold. A sheer gold ribbon hangs this wreath on the door and dresses it up too.

If silver suits your fancy more, then so be it. It is the effect of metallic luster on natural material that just makes a wreath such as this so enchanting. Season after season, these wreaths can be used and reused—as long as there is always a little bit of paint!

SOME ARE SILVER, SOME ARE GOLD

A festival of complements, this wreath strikes a dynamic chord with its varying tones of silver and gold set on a rustic grape vine and willow twig form. Using both silver and gold makes a fine paring, and equally attractive is using natural and painted cones too. If committing to an all-silver or all-gold wreath is too tough a decision, then this wreath may be your best choice. From the dawning of the holiday season to the setting of the winter sun, a wreath such as this can bring a bit of glamour to your door. Rustic base and elements mixed with fancier golds and silver—such an agreeable combo.

ROSEMARY AND CITRUS What a wreath for the senses! The visual comforts this wreath affords are only a part of its attributes. Its fragrant elements just may be the best combo I know. Earthy headed magnolia and seeded eucalyptus commence the olfactory orchestra. Then rosemary, with its slightly sweet yet piney aroma, melds with the fragrance of citrus—Meyer lemons in this case. The peppery slant these lemons' perfume emits along with the strength and freshness of the rosemary is simply delicious to smell and highly flavorful for cooking too. A twist in this bouquet of scents is cinnamon, and it makes a pleasant visual component as well.

I truly believe this wreath is fine and attractive enough without a ribbon, so the cinnamon sticks act as the "bow." Crossed and pinned with a lemon half, the cinnamon sticks anchor the wreath, adding a touch of earthen color and rustic charm. If I could bottle up a wreath to smell for days to come, this wreath would be top contender.

TRADITION WITH A TWIST Red and green are the epitome of our holiday color scheme and rightly so, for the majority of our evergreens produce a profusion of red berries this time of year. The ability to take a simple wreath and elaborate upon it with garden jewels is one of my favorite things.

Starting with a plain Fraser fir wreath and adding some dimension with white pine boughs is the first step to revving up the visual appeal. Red nandina berries and the russet and burgundy hued foliage of the nandina also add dramatic contrast against the greenery.

Yet, as this season is upon us and the garden is offering heavy doses of red and green, a nod to the seasons past gives this traditional wreath a twist on tradition. Dried hydrangeas, with their fading blue of glorious summer days, tucked into the greenery and set against the red berries makes a wreath that is striking in its contrasts and complements of texture and tone. Marrying the best of summer's bounty with winter's own charms is just the way to create a wreath full of appeal.

For added texture, I like preserved lichen, moss or sponge mushrooms. These fanning fungi give not only the texture that makes these wreaths appealing, but also a dose of earthen zip and dimension. Movement and dimension are key elements to a wreath's makeup, and a collection of wreath essentials, such as berries, fungi, foliage and blossoms in this case, makes for a wreath worthy of celebrating any event during the season.

MAGNOLIA MAVEN This type of magnolia wreath, with a base form of counterclockwise leaves, is stunning on its own. Add in some of the wintertime's best garden contributions, and a wreath worthy of endless holiday season is at hand. Besides such a great shape and outline, the magnolia leaf is extra versatile with its sienna-shaded back. Immediately, tone and contrast are set just by using this two-toned bit of foliage. Add in another greenery for more texture, Cryptomeria in this instance, and a gorgeous wreath of greens may now adorn your home's entrance. But a bit of red never hurts this time year either, so holly berries from the dwarf Burford and Winterberry shrubs turn this wreath into the classic color scheme we expect for this season.

ROSES AND ROSEMARY Just hearing the combo of sweetly scented roses paired with piney evergreen rosemary is enough to delight the senses. Add in the scents, shapes and textures of different citrus, and you have a wreath fit for Christmastime through Valentine's. Reds, greens, yellows, oranges and corals all take their color cues from one another and fill this wreath with the utmost of amazing scents, visual appeasement and tactile enchantment too.

Beginning with a base of boxwood, sprigs of rosemary are tucked into the foliage form, creating first a contrast of foliage colors and textures. Second, halves of Meyer lemons and grapefruits are staked into the boxwood form. These bursts of citrus are so apropos for a wintertime wreath, since citrus is a winter crop coming from the Gulf Coast states and California. Red roses then fill the gaps with a velvety depth and marvelous floral touch. Different colors of roses, such as yellow or orange, could also be used. Hang this wreath for your holiday fest or create it for your Valentine's Day dinner; in either month this wreath will delight all the senses.

CONES AND PODS

Varying colors of brown, burnt sienna, copper and rust all meld together with varying textures for this wintertime wreath. Pinecones in an assortment of sizes and shapes fit around and are glued to a foam wreath form. Some are lightly lacquered and others left natural. The slight addition of a few popcorn berries and a taupe-hued velvet bow further enhance the "shades of brown" color scheme and textural array.

A wreath such as this will last for years, and the ribbon can be changed to give it festive charm from Thanksgiving on through winter. The absence of greenery, and thus the strength of the browns, is what makes this wreath so appealing. Whether it finds its way onto a door or armoire, this wreath will surely be an outward sign of your welcoming the season.